RECORDED VERSIONS GUITAR®

AUTHENTIC TRANSCRIPTIONS
WITH NOTES AND TABLATURE

Transcribed by
**STEVE GORENBERG**
and
**TROY NELSON**

# silverchair
## FREAK SHOW

ISBN 0-7935-7230-4

HAL•LEONARD®
CORPORATION

7777 W. BLUEMOUND RD. P.O. BOX 13819 MILWAUKEE, WI 53213

Visit Hal Leonard Online at
**www.halleonard.com**

# silverchair
## FREAK SHOW

# Slave

**Words by Daniel Johns**
**Music by Daniel Johns and Ben Gillies**

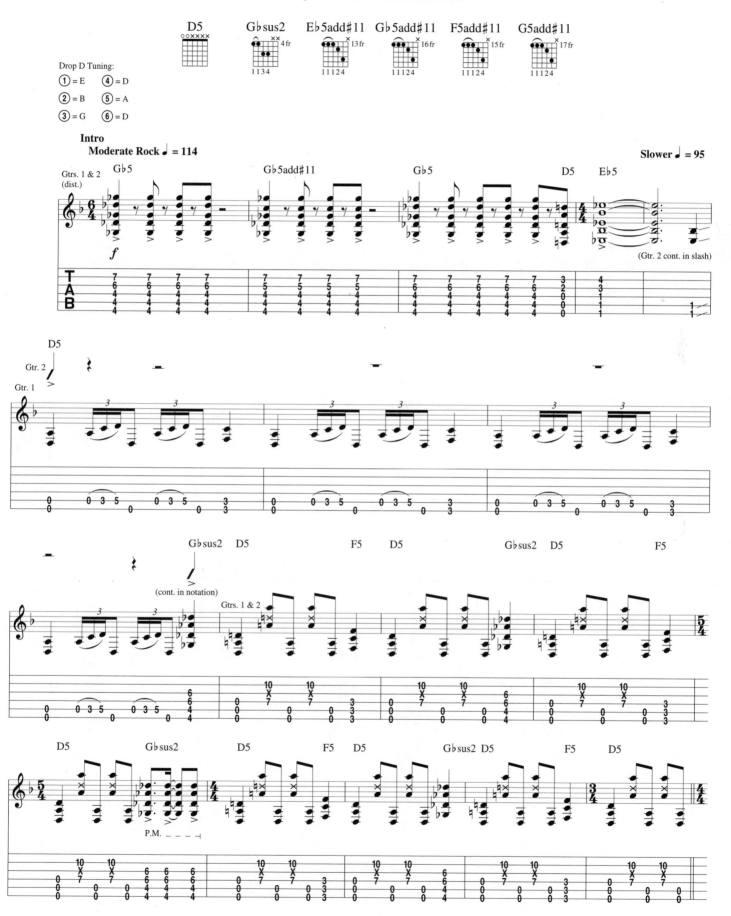

**Verse**

1. Lived too long, now you've come __ to take __ me to _____ a place where I _____ can die. _____

Gtrs. 1 & 2: w/ Rhy. Fig. 1

Lost my soul, lost my con - fi - dence _ in me. _____ Can't be some-thing, but __ I'll try.

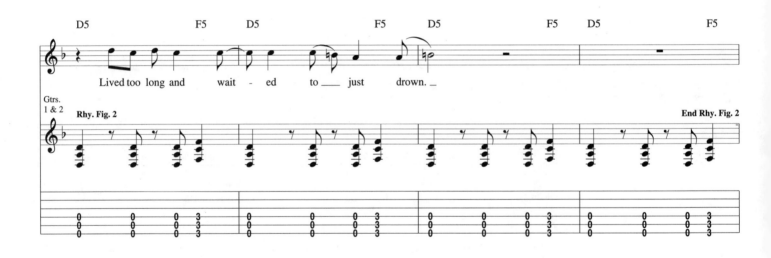

Lived too long and wait - ed to __ just drown. _

Gtrs. 1 & 2: w/ Rhy. Fig. 2, 1st 3 meas.

In my self pit - y, I _____ keep fall - ing down. _____

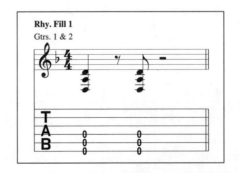

**Interlude**

E5 Eb5 D5 E5 Eb5 D5 E5 Eb5 D5 E5 Eb5 D5 E5 Eb5 D5

**Double-Time Feel**

C5 B5 D5 C5 B5 D5 C5 B5 D5 C5 B5 D5 C5 D5 Bbsus2

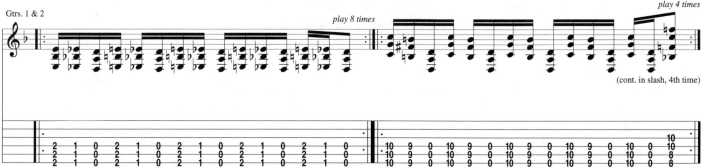

**Outro**

Eb5add#11

I can't find. _  I can't find. _  I can't find. _  I can't find. _

Gb5add#11                                    F5add#11

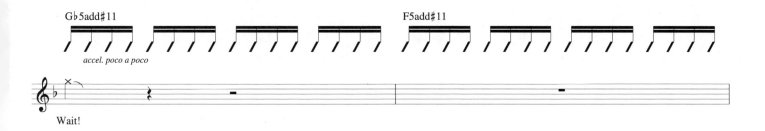

Wait!

G5add#11

**End Double-Time Feel    Slower ♩ = 95**

G5add#11                                    D5  N.C.          F5      D5

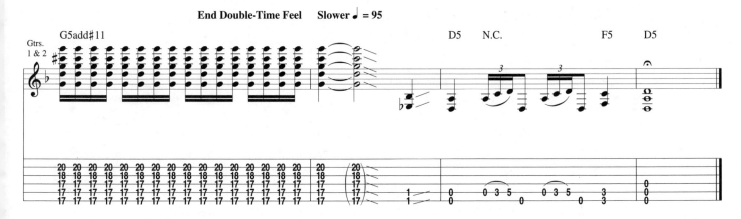

# Freak

**Words and Music by Daniel Johns**

# Abuse Me

**Words and Music by Daniel Johns**

Noth - ing ___ seems to both - er. Wish I ___ had a clue. ___
No one seems to like ___ you. Wish I ___ could - n't tell.

**Chorus**

C' - mon, ___ a - buse me more, I ___ like ___ it. ___

# Lie to Me

**Words and Music by Daniel Johns**

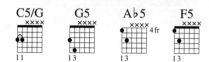

**Intro**
**Fast Rock** ♩ = 188

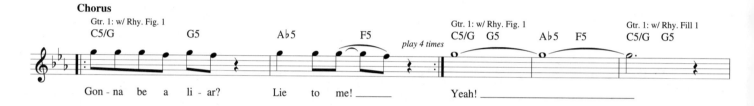

**Chorus**

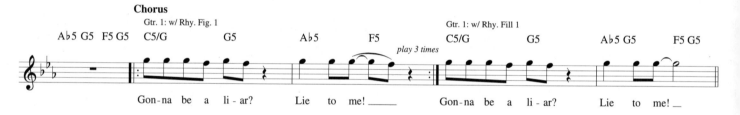

Gon - na be a li - ar? Lie to me! _____ Yeah! _____

**Chorus**

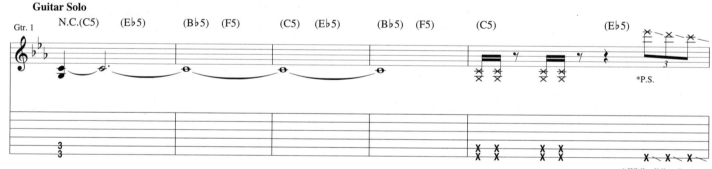

Gon - na be a li - ar? Lie to me! _____ Gon-na be a li - ar? Lie to me! _

**Guitar Solo**

* While sliding down str.
bounce edge of pick in
rhythm indicated.

**Rhy. Fill 1**

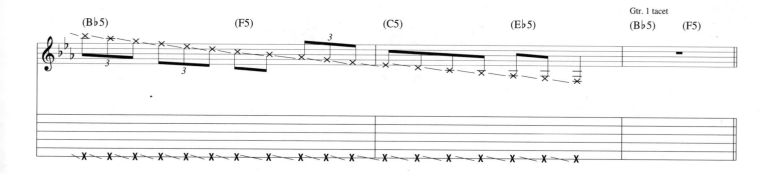

**Chorus**

Gon - na be a - while? Lie to me. _____

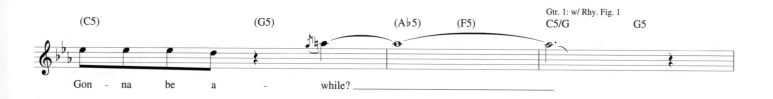

Gon - na be a - while? _____

**Outro**

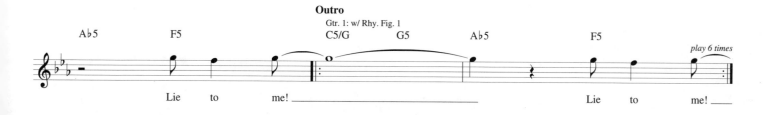

Lie to me! _____ Lie to me! _____

**Free Time**

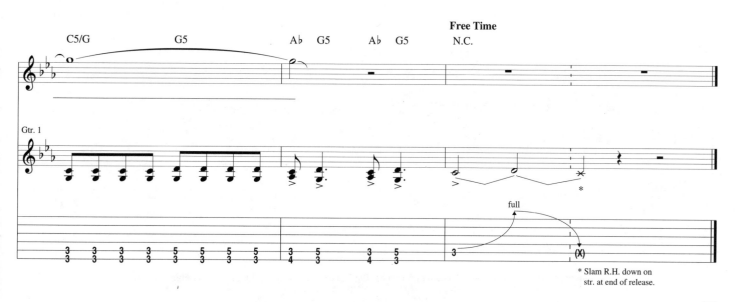

\* Slam R.H. down on
str. at end of release.

# No Association

**Words by Daniel Johns**
**Music by Daniel Johns and Ben Gillies**

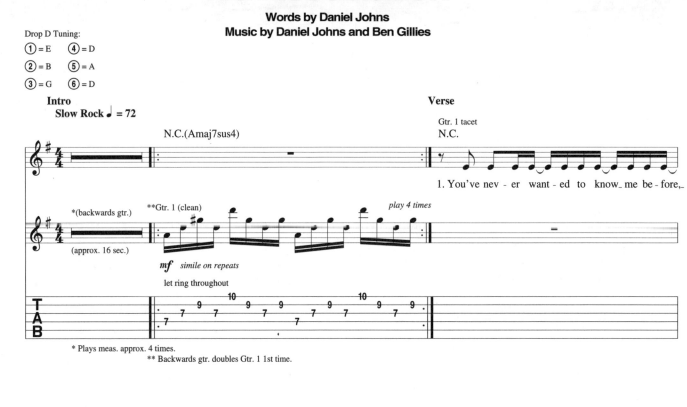

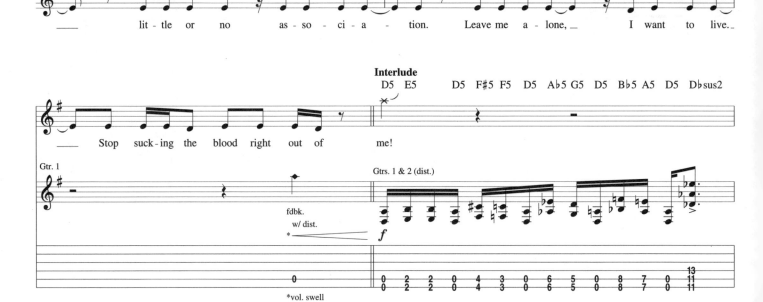

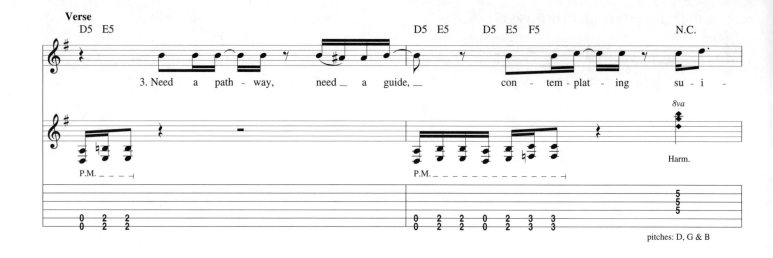

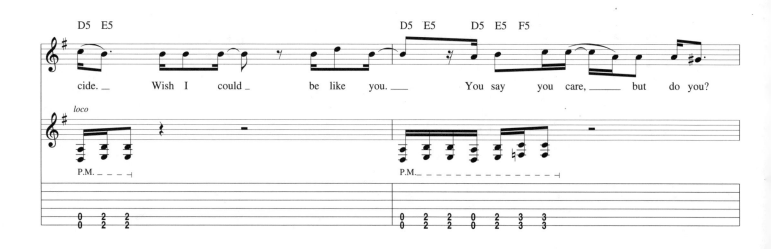

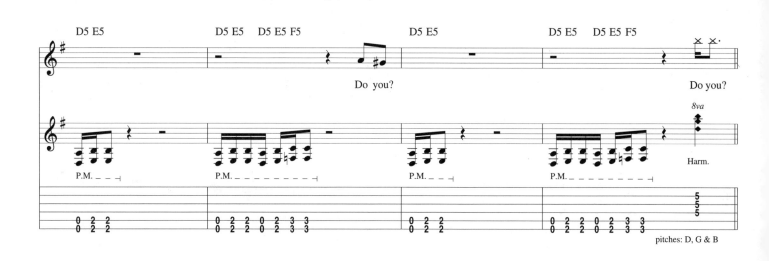

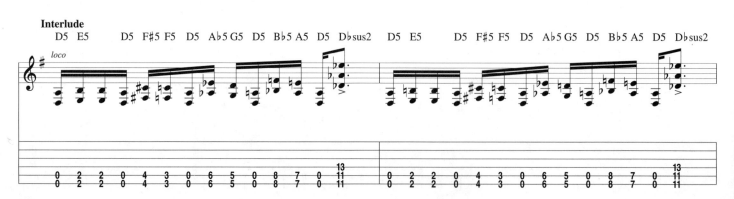

# Cemetery

**Words and Music by Daniel Johns**

31

# The Door

**Words and Music by Daniel Johns**

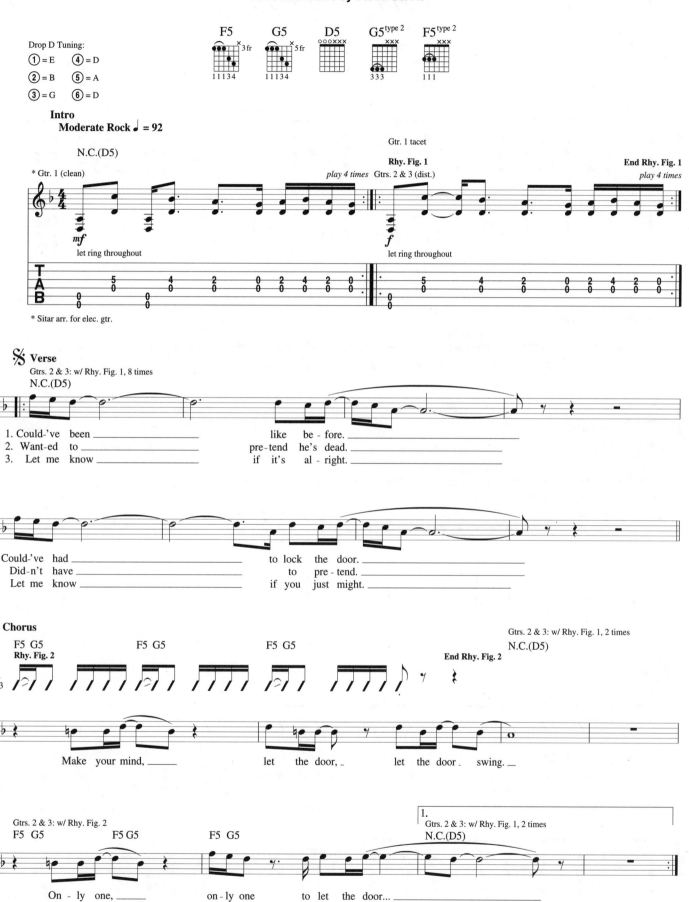

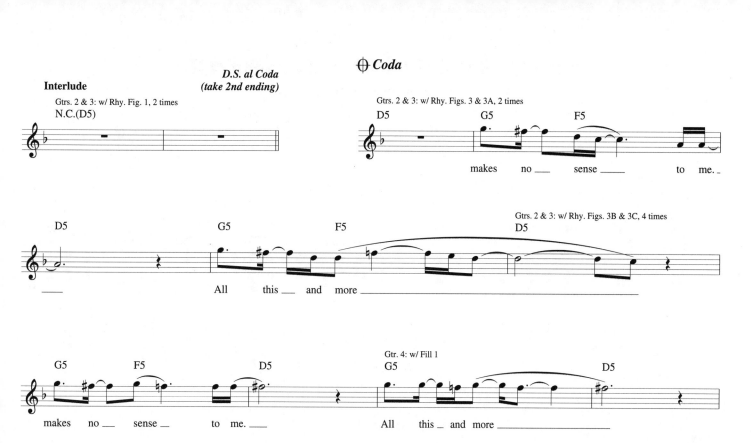

# Pop Song for Us Rejects

**Words and Music by Daniel Johns**

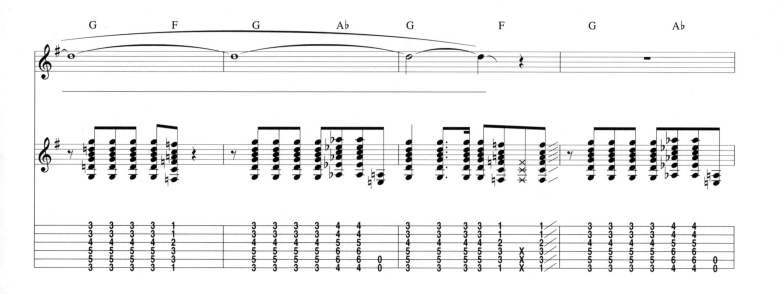

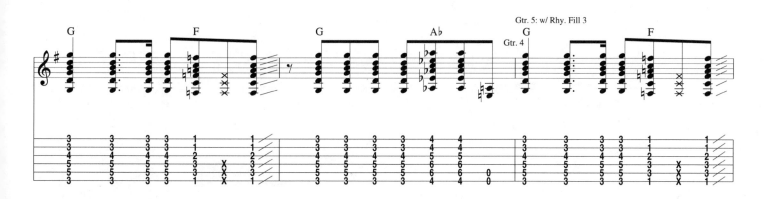

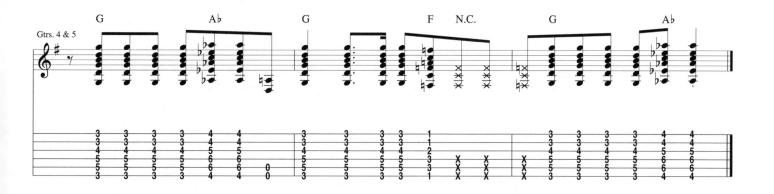

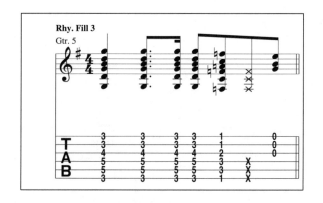

# Learn to Hate

**Words by Daniel Johns**
**Music by Ben Gillies**

# Petrol & Chlorine

### Words and Music by Daniel Johns

Open C Tuning:
① = C  ④ = C
② = G  ⑤ = G
③ = E  ⑥ = C

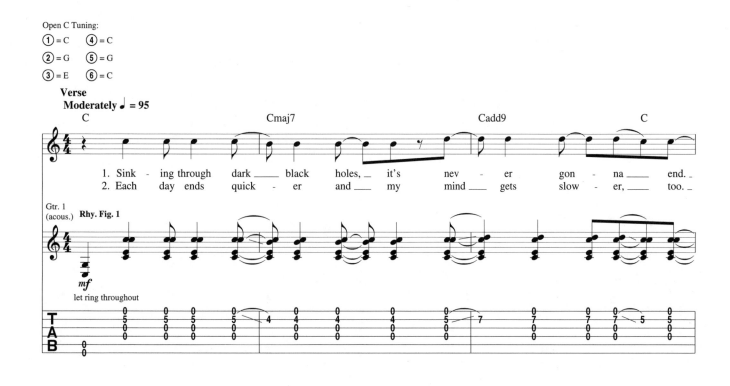

**Verse**
**Moderately** ♩ = 95

1. Sink - ing through dark ___ black holes, ___ it's nev - er gon - na ___ end. ___
2. Each day ends quick - er and ___ my mind ___ gets slow - er, ___ too. ___

Gtr. 1 (acous.) **Rhy. Fig. 1**

*mf*
let ring throughout

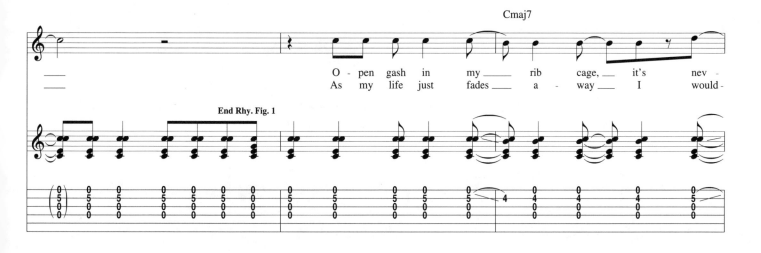

O - pen gash in my ___ rib cage, ___ it's nev -
As my life just fades ___ a - way ___ I would -

End Rhy. Fig. 1

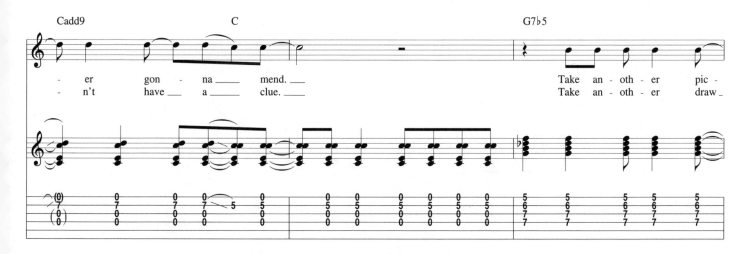

- er gon - na ___ mend. ___
- n't have ___ a ___ clue. ___

Take an - oth - er pic -
Take an - oth - er draw

**Interlude**

Gtr. 2 tacet

N.C.(C)

Gtr. 1

Rhy. Fig. 3                                                                              End Rhy. Fig. 3

Gtr. 1: w/ Rhy. Fig. 3, 2 times

Mm. _____

**Chorus**

C                                         E♭6                              D7sus4

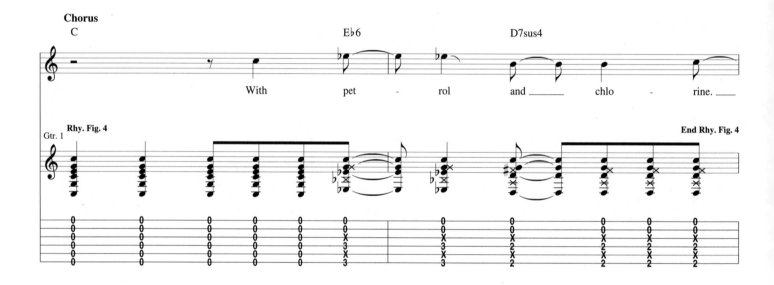

With          pet -        rol          and _____ chlo -        rine. ____

Gtr. 1

Rhy. Fig. 4                                                                              End Rhy. Fig. 4

Gtr. 1: w/ Rhy. Fig. 2, 2 times

C        D7sus4  E♭6                              D7sus4              C        N.C.(C)

_____   You ____ could    see ____ it,    I _____ was    blind. _____

C        D7sus4  E♭6                              D7sus4              C        N.C.(C)

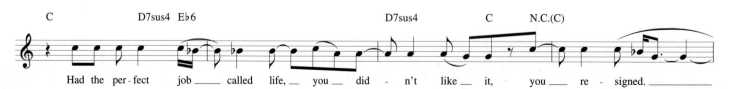

Had the per-fect    job ____ called  life, ___ you ___ did - n't    like ___ it,    you ___ re - signed. _____

Gtr. 1: w/ Rhy. Fig. 4, 4 times

With pet - rol and chlo - rine, you know just what I mean.

With pet - rol and chlo - rine, you know just what I mean.

**Outro**

Gtr. 3: w/ Fill 4

N.C.(C)

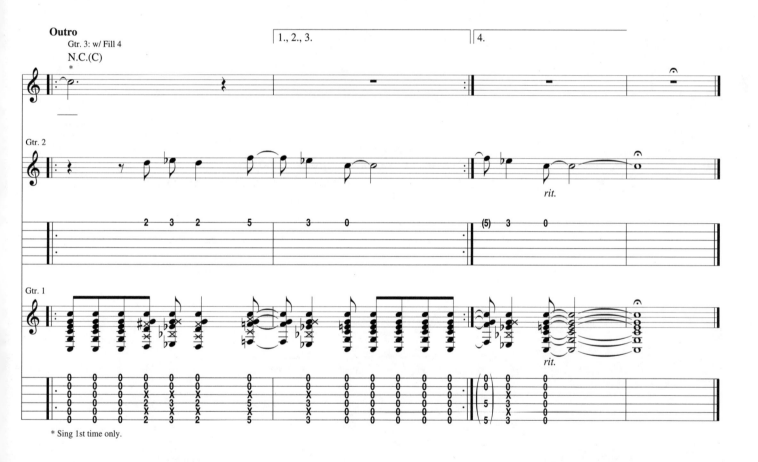

\* Sing 1st time only.

**Fill 4**

Gtr. 3 (acous.)

play 3 times

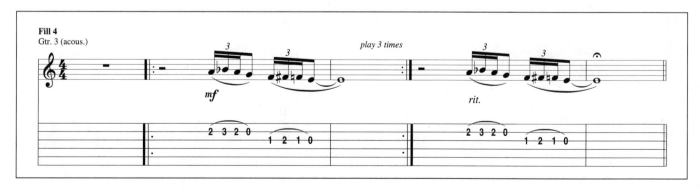

# Roses

**Words by Daniel Johns**
**Music by Daniel Johns and Ben Gillies**

# Nobody Came

**Words by Daniel Johns**

**Music by Daniel Johns and Ben Gillies**

Interlude

Verse
Half-Time Feel

2. His father beats him, no hesitation. Face left dripping in humiliation.

Chorus

Head's a crying wasteland filled with shame. Cried for help before and nobody came.

Interlude

Oh.

* Gtr. 1 uses dist. during 3rd & 4th meas. of Rhy. Fig. 3.    ** bass plays E♭

Verse
Half-Time Feel

3. As he lies wounded his father turns to clay. A frozen statue can't walk away.

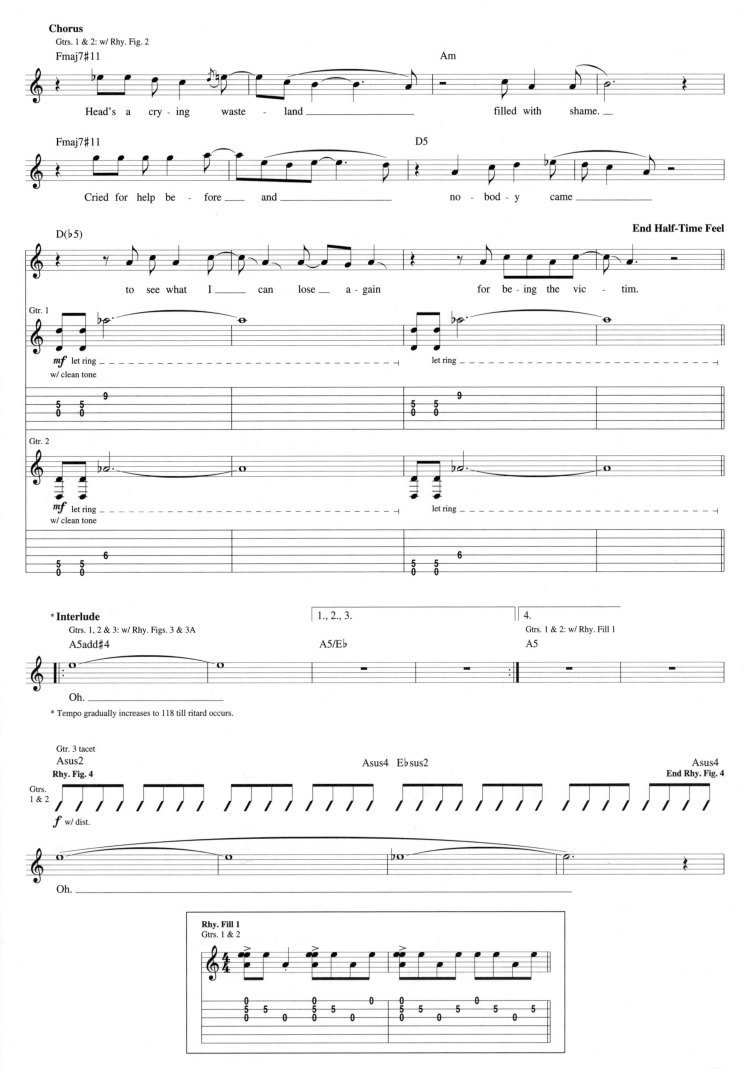

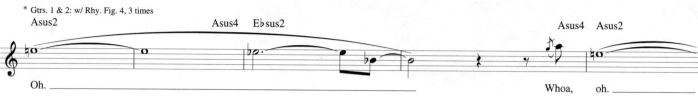

**Guitar Solo**

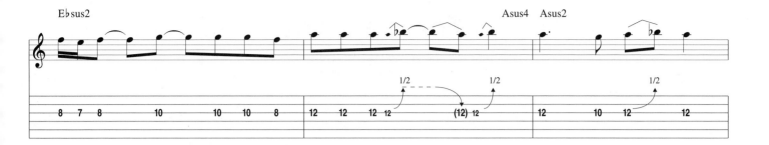

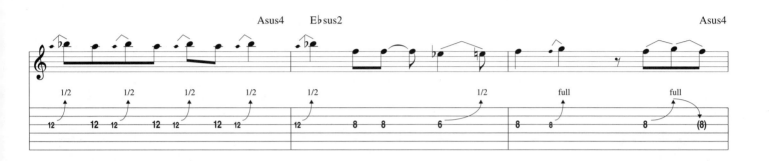

\* Bend string behind nut.

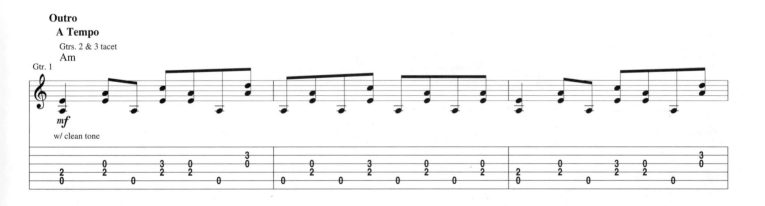

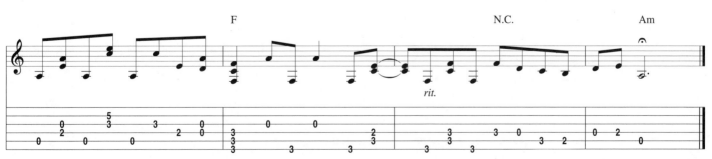

# The Closing

**Words by Daniel Johns**
**Music by Ben Gillies**

# Guitar Notation Legend

Guitar Music can be notated three different ways: on a *musical staff*, in *tablature*, and in *rhythm slashes*.

**RHYTHM SLASHES** are written above the staff. Strum chords in the rhythm indicated. Use the chord diagrams found at the top of the first page of the transcription for the appropriate chord voicings. Round noteheads indicate single notes.

**THE MUSICAL STAFF** shows pitches and rhythms and is divided by bar lines into measures. Pitches are named after the first seven letters of the alphabet.

**TABLATURE** graphically represents the guitar fingerboard. Each horizontal line represents a a string, and each number represents a fret.

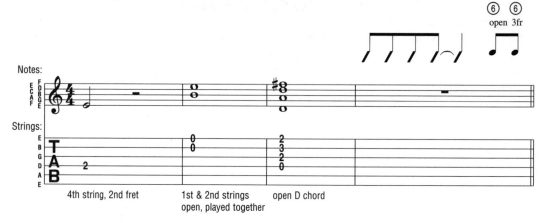

4th string, 2nd fret

1st & 2nd strings open, played together

open D chord

# Definitions for Special Guitar Notation

**HALF-STEP BEND:** Strike the note and bend up 1/2 step.

**WHOLE-STEP BEND:** Strike the note and bend up one step.

**GRACE NOTE BEND:** Strike the note and bend up as indicated. The first note does not take up any time.

**SLIGHT (MICROTONE) BEND:** Strike the note and bend up 1/4 step.

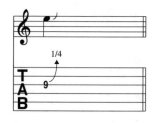

**BEND AND RELEASE:** Strike the note and bend up as indicated, then release back to the original note. Only the first note is struck.

**PRE-BEND:** Bend the note as indicated, then strike it.

**PRE-BEND AND RELEASE:** Bend the note as indicated. Strike it and release the bend back to the original note.

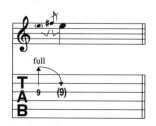

**UNISON BEND:** Strike the two notes simultaneously and bend the lower note up to the pitch of the higher.

**VIBRATO:** The string is vibrated by rapidly bending and releasing the note with the fretting hand.

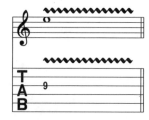

**WIDE VIBRATO:** The pitch is varied to a greater degree by vibrating with the fretting hand.

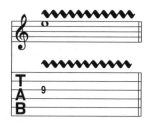

**HAMMER-ON:** Strike the first (lower) note with one finger, then sound the higher note (on the same string) with another finger by fretting it without picking.

**PULL-OFF:** Place both fingers on the notes to be sounded. Strike the first note and without picking, pull the finger off to sound the second (lower) note.

**LEGATO SLIDE:** Strike the first note and then slide the same fret-hand finger up or down to the second note. The second note is not struck.

**SHIFT SLIDE:** Same as legato slide, except the second note is struck.

**TRILL:** Very rapidly alternate between the notes indicated by continuously hammering on and pulling off.

**TAPPING:** Hammer ("tap") the fret indicated with the pick-hand index or middle finger and pull off to the note fretted by the fret hand.

**NATURAL HARMONIC:** Strike the note while the fret-hand lightly touches the string directly over the fret indicated.

**PINCH HARMONIC:** The note is fretted normally and a harmonic is produced by adding the edge of the thumb or the tip of the index finger of the pick hand to the normal pick attack.

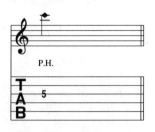

**HARP HARMONIC:** The note is fretted normally and a harmonic is produced by gently resting the pick hand's index finger directly above the indicated fret (in parentheses) while the pick hand's thumb or pick assists by plucking the appropriate string.

**PICK SCRAPE:** The edge of the pick is rubbed down (or up) the string, producing a scratchy sound.

**MUFFLED STRINGS:** A percussive sound is produced by laying the fret hand across the string(s) without depressing, and striking them with the pick hand.

**PALM MUTING:** The note is partially muted by the pick hand lightly touching the string(s) just before the bridge.

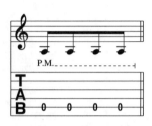

**RAKE:** Drag the pick across the strings indicated with a single motion.

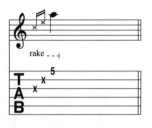

**TREMOLO PICKING:** The note is picked as rapidly and continuously as possible.

**ARPEGGIATE:** Play the notes of the chord indicated by quickly rolling them from bottom to top.

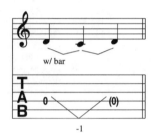

**VIBRATO BAR DIVE AND RETURN:** The pitch of the note or chord is dropped a specified number of steps (in rhythm) then returned to the original pitch.

**VIBRATO BAR SCOOP:** Depress the bar just before striking the note, then quickly release the bar.

**VIBRATO BAR DIP:** Strike the note and then immediately drop a specified number of steps, then release back to the original pitch.

# Additional Musical Definitions

 *(accent)* • Accentuate note (play it louder)

 *(accent)* • Accentuate note with great intensity

 *(staccato)* • Play the note short

 • Downstroke

V • Upstroke

***D.S. al Coda*** • Go back to the sign ( 𝄋 ), then play until the measure marked "**To Coda**," then skip to the section labelled "**Coda**."

***D.S. al Fine*** • Go back to the beginning of the song and play until the measure marked "***Fine***" (end).

**Rhy. Fig.** • Label used to recall a recurring accompaniment pattern (usually chordal).

**Riff** • Label used to recall composed, melodic lines (usually single notes) which recur.

**Fill** • Label used to identify a brief melodic figure which is to be inserted into the arrangement.

**Rhy. Fill** • A chordal version of a Fill.

**tacet** • Instrument is silent (drops out).

 • Repeat measures between signs.

 • When a repeated section has different endings, play the first ending only the first time and the second ending only the second time.

**NOTE:** Tablature numbers in parentheses mean:
1. The note is being sustained over a system (note in standard notation is tied), or
2. The note is sustained, but a new articulation (such as a hammer-on, pull-off, slide or vibrato begins, or
3. The note is a barely audible "ghost" note (note in standard notation is also in parentheses).

# RECORDED VERSIONS

## *The Best Note-For-Note Transcriptions Available*

**ALL BOOKS INCLUDE TABLATURE**

| | | |
|---|---|---|
| 00690002 | Aerosmith – Big Ones | $24.95 |
| 00694909 | Aerosmith – Get A Grip | $19.95 |
| 00660133 | Aerosmith – Pump | $19.95 |
| 00690139 | Alice In Chains | $19.95 |
| 00694865 | Alice In Chains – Dirt | $19.95 |
| 00660225 | Alice In Chains – Facelift | $19.95 |
| 00694925 | Alice In Chains – Jar Of Flies/Sap | $19.95 |
| 00694932 | Allman Brothers Band – Volume 1 | $24.95 |
| 00694933 | Allman Brothers Band – Volume 2 | $24.95 |
| 00694934 | Allman Brothers Band – Volume 3 | $24.95 |
| 00690158 | Chet Atkins – Almost Alone | $19.95 |
| 00694877 | Chet Atkins – Guitars For All Seasons | $19.95 |
| 00694918 | Randy Bachman Collection | $22.95 |
| 00694929 | Beatles: 1962-1966 | $24.95 |
| 00694930 | Beatles: 1967-1970 | $24.95 |
| 00694880 | Beatles – Abbey Road | $19.95 |
| 00690044 | Beatles – Live At The BBC | $22.95 |
| 00694891 | Beatles – Revolver | $19.95 |
| 00694914 | Beatles – Rubber Soul | $19.95 |
| 00694863 | Beatles – Sgt. Pepper's Lonely Hearts Club Band | $19.95 |
| 00690174 | Beck – Mellow Gold | $17.95 |
| 00690175 | Beck – Odelay | $17.95 |
| 00694931 | Belly – Star | $19.95 |
| 00694884 | The Best of George Benson | $19.95 |
| 00692385 | Chuck Berry | $19.95 |
| 00692200 | Black Sabbath – We Sold Our Soul For Rock 'N' Roll | $19.95 |
| 00690115 | Blind Melon – Soup | $19.95 |
| 00690028 | Blue Oyster Cult – Cult Classics | $19.95 |
| 00690102 | Bon Jovi – These Days | $24.95 |
| 00690173 | Tracy Bonham – The Burdens Of Being Upright | $19.95 |
| 00694935 | Boston: Double Shot Of | $22.95 |
| 00690043 | Cheap Trick – Best Of | $19.95 |
| 00306124 | Chicago – The Retrospective Collection | $22.95 |
| 00694875 | Eric Clapton – Boxed Set | $75.00 |
| 00692392 | Eric Clapton – Crossroads Vol. 1 | $22.95 |
| 00692393 | Eric Clapton – Crossroads Vol. 2 | $22.95 |
| 00692394 | Eric Clapton – Crossroads Vol. 3 | $22.95 |
| 00690010 | Eric Clapton – From The Cradle | $19.95 |
| 00660139 | Eric Clapton – Journeyman | $19.95 |
| 00694869 | Eric Clapton – Live Acoustic | $19.95 |
| 00694873 | Eric Clapton – Timepieces | $19.95 |
| 00694896 | John Mayall/Eric Clapton – Bluesbreakers | $19.95 |
| 00694837 | Albert Collins – The Complete Imperial Records | $19.95 |
| 00694941 | Crash Test Dummies – God Shuffled His Feet | $19.95 |
| 00694840 | Cream – Disraeli Gears | $19.95 |
| 00690007 | Danzig 4 | $19.95 |
| 00690184 | DC Talk – Jesus Freak | $19.95 |
| 00660186 | Alex De Grassi Guitar Collection | $19.95 |
| 00694831 | Derek And The Dominos – Layla & Other Assorted Love Songs | $19.95 |
| 00690187 | Dire Straits – Brothers In Arms | $19.95 |
| 00690191 | Dire Straits – Money For Nothing | $24.95 |
| 00690182 | Dishwalla – Pet Your Friends | $19.95 |
| 00660178 | Willie Dixon – Master Blues Composer | $24.95 |
| 00690089 | Foo Fighters | $19.95 |
| 00690042 | Robben Ford Blues Collection | $19.95 |
| 00694920 | Free – Best Of | $18.95 |
| 00694894 | Frank Gambale – The Great Explorers | $19.95 |
| 00694807 | Danny Gatton – 88 Elmira St | $19.95 |
| 00690127 | Goo Goo Dolls – A Boy Named Goo | $19.95 |
| 00690117 | John Gorka Collection | $19.95 |
| 00690114 | Buddy Guy Collection Vol. A-J | $19.95 |

| | | |
|---|---|---|
| 00690193 | Buddy Guy Collection Vol. L-Y | $19.95 |
| 00694798 | George Harrison Anthology | $19.95 |
| 00690068 | Return Of The Hellecasters | $19.95 |
| 00692930 | Jimi Hendrix – Are You Experienced? | $19.95 |
| 00692931 | Jimi Hendrix – Axis: Bold As Love | $19.95 |
| 00694944 | Jimi Hendrix – Blues | $24.95 |
| 00660192 | The Jimi Hendrix – Concerts | $24.95 |
| 00692932 | Jimi Hendrix – Electric Ladyland | $24.95 |
| 00660099 | Jimi Hendrix – Radio One | $24.95 |
| 00694919 | Jimi Hendrix – Stone Free | $19.95 |
| 00690017 | Jimi Hendrix – Woodstock | $24.95 |
| 00690038 | Gary Hoey – Best Of | $19.95 |
| 00660029 | Buddy Holly | $19.95 |
| 00660200 | John Lee Hooker – The Healer | $19.95 |
| 00660169 | John Lee Hooker – A Blues Legend | $19.95 |
| 00694054 | Hootie & The Blowfish – Cracked Rear View | $19.95 |
| 00690143 | Hootie & The Blowfish – Fairweather Johnson | $19.95 |
| 00694905 | Howlin' Wolf | $19.95 |
| 00690136 | Indigo Girls – 1200 Curfews | $19.95 |
| 00694938 | Elmore James – Master Electric Slide Guitar | $19.95 |
| 00694833 | Billy Joel For Guitar | $19.95 |
| 00694912 | Eric Johnson – Ah Via Musicom | $19.95 |
| 00694911 | Eric Johnson – Tones | $19.95 |
| 00690169 | Eric Johnson – Venus Isle | $19.95 |
| 00694799 | Robert Johnson – At The Crossroads | $19.95 |
| 00693185 | Judas Priest – Vintage Hits | $19.95 |
| 00690073 | B. B. King – 1950-1957 | $24.95 |
| 00690098 | B. B. King – 1958-1967 | $24.95 |
| 00690099 | B. B. King – 1962-1971 | $24.95 |
| 00690019 | King's X – Best Of | $19.95 |
| 00694903 | The Best Of Kiss | $24.95 |
| 00690163 | Mark Knopfler/Chet Atkins – Neck and Neck | $19.95 |
| 00690070 | Live – Throwing Copper | $19.95 |
| 00690018 | Living Colour – Best Of | $19.95 |
| 00694954 | Lynyrd Skynyrd, New Best Of | $19.95 |
| 00694845 | Yngwie Malmsteen – Fire And Ice | $19.95 |
| 00690190 | Marilyn Manson – Antichrist Superstar | $19.95 |
| 00694956 | Bob Marley – Legend | $19.95 |
| 00690075 | Bob Marley – Natural Mystic | $19.95 |
| 00690020 | Meat Loaf – Bat Out Of Hell I & II | $22.95 |
| 00694951 | Megadeth – Rust In Peace | $22.95 |
| 00690011 | Megadeath – Youthanasia | $19.95 |
| 00690040 | Steve Miller Band Greatest Hits | $19.95 |
| 00694868 | Gary Moore – After Hours | $19.95 |
| 00694802 | Gary Moore – Still Got The Blues | $19.95 |
| 00690103 | Alanis Morissette – Jagged Little Pill | $19.95 |
| 00694958 | Mountain, Best Of | $19.95 |
| 00694895 | Nirvana – Bleach | $19.95 |
| 00690189 | Nirvana – From The Muddy Banks of the Wishkah | $19.95 |
| 00694913 | Nirvana – In Utero | $19.95 |
| 00694901 | Nirvana – Incesticide | $19.95 |
| 00694883 | Nirvana – Nevermind | $19.95 |
| 00690026 | Nirvana – Unplugged In New York | $19.95 |
| 00690159 | Oasis – Definitely Maybe | $19.95 |
| 00690121 | Oasis – (What's The Story) Morning Glory | $19.95 |
| 00694830 | Ozzy Osbourne – No More Tears | $19.95 |
| 00690129 | Ozzy Osbourne – Ozzmosis | $22.95 |
| 00694855 | Pearl Jam – Ten | $19.95 |
| 00690053 | Liz Phair – Whip Smart | $19.95 |
| 00690176 | Phish – Billy Breathes | $22.95 |
| 00693800 | Pink Floyd – Early Classics | $19.95 |
| 00694967 | Police – Message In A Box Boxed Set | $70.00 |

| | | |
|---|---|---|
| 00690032 | Elvis Presley – The Sun Sessions | $22.95 |
| 00694974 | Queen – A Night At The Opera | $19.95 |
| 00694969 | Queensryche – Selections from "Operation: Mindcrime" | $19.95 |
| 00694910 | Rage Against The Machine | $19.95 |
| 00690145 | Rage Against The Machine – Evil Empire | $19.95 |
| 00690055 | Red Hot Chili Peppers – Bloodsugarsexmagik | $19.95 |
| 00690090 | Red Hot Chili Peppers – One Hot Minute | $22.95 |
| 00690027 | Red Hot Chili Peppers – Out In L.A. | $19.95 |
| 00694968 | Red Hot Chili Peppers – Selections from "What Hits!?" | $22.95 |
| 00694892 | Guitar Style Of Jerry Reed | $19.95 |
| 00694937 | Jimmy Reed – Master Bluesman | $19.95 |
| 00694899 | R.E.M. – Automatic For The People | $19.95 |
| 00694898 | R.E.M. – Out Of Time | $19.95 |
| 00690014 | Rolling Stones – Exile On Main Street | $24.95 |
| 00690186 | Rolling Stones – Rock & Roll Circus | $19.95 |
| 00694976 | Rolling Stones – Some Girls | $24.95 |
| 00690133 | Rusted Root – When I Woke | $19.95 |
| 00694836 | Richie Sambora – Stranger In This Town | $19.95 |
| 00690031 | Santana's Greatest Hits | $19.95 |
| 00694805 | Scorpions – Crazy World | $19.95 |
| 00694916 | Scorpions – Face The Heat | $19.95 |
| 00690128 | Seven Mary Three – American Standards | $19.95 |
| 00690076 | Sex Pistols – Never Mind The Bollocks | $19.95 |
| 00690130 | Silverchair – Frogstomp | $19.95 |
| 00690041 | Smithereens – Best Of | $19.95 |
| 00694885 | Spin Doctors – Pocket Full Of Kryptonite | $19.95 |
| 00120004 | Steely Dan – Best Of | $24.95 |
| 00694921 | Steppenwolf, The Best Of | $22.95 |
| 00694957 | Rod Stewart – Unplugged...And Seated | $22.95 |
| 00690021 | Sting – Fields Of Gold | $19.95 |
| 00694824 | Best Of James Taylor | $16.95 |
| 00694887 | Thin Lizzy – The Best Of Thin Lizzy | $19.95 |
| 00690022 | Richard Thompson Guitar | $19.95 |
| 00690030 | Toad The Wet Sprocket | $19.95 |
| 00694411 | U2 – The Joshua Tree | $19.95 |
| 00690039 | Steve Vai – Alien Love Secrets | $24.95 |
| 00690172 | Steve Vai – Fire Garden | $22.95 |
| 00660137 | Steve Vai – Passion & Warfare | $24.95 |
| 00694904 | Vai – Sex and Religion | $24.95 |
| 00690023 | Jimmie Vaughan – Strange Pleasures | $19.95 |
| 00690024 | Stevie Ray Vaughan – Couldn't Stand The Weather | $19.95 |
| 00660136 | Stevie Ray Vaughan – In Step | $19.95 |
| 00694879 | Stevie Ray Vaughan – In The Beginning | $19.95 |
| 00690036 | Stevie Ray Vaughan – Live Alive | $24.95 |
| 00694835 | Stevie Ray Vaughan – The Sky Is Crying | $19.95 |
| 00690025 | Stevie Ray Vaughan – Soul To Soul | $19.95 |
| 00690015 | Stevie Ray Vaughan – Texas Flood | $19.95 |
| 00694776 | Vaughan Brothers – Family Style | $19.95 |
| 00120026 | Joe Walsh – Look What I Did... | $24.95 |
| 00694789 | Muddy Waters – Deep Blues | $24.95 |
| 00690071 | Weezer | $19.95 |